RETURN TO EDEN

A Spiritual Path to Your Divine Ascension

Jason E. Reider

Printed in the United States of America

ISBN: 978-0-578-40584-1

Cover Design: Rick Soldin
Text Design and Composition: Rick Soldin

Cover Image: johnwoodcockillustration.co.uk

For all seekers of truth, joy and harmony.

You are already what you seek.

For Kelly, Keira and Blake.

May you invariably be conscious of

MY peace that is always within you.

In loving memory of a true friend Michael E. Strouse.

Thank you for teaching me how to choose joy.

Contents

Acknowledgments 7

Introduction 9

Eden Lost 13

The Need for Eden 21

The Key to Eden 29

Traveling Down the Path 37

Living in Eden 47

Spiritual Health 57

Leading Others to Eden 65

Christ and Christ Consciousness 73

The Dream of Reality 81

Crucify Your Ego 87

Welcome to Eden 95

Seven Keys to the Mastery of Christ Consciousness

1

Realize and accept the fullness of God's Omnipresence. There is a Spiritual universe. Spirit is the substance of life. Life therefore is infinite, perfect, indestructible and there is no other life besides the Life of God.

Acknowledgments

*F*irst and foremost, I thank God, the One power that is within all of us. Thank you, Father, for guiding and communing with me during my rapid spiritual development. I thank you for working from within everyone that has ever crossed paths with me and may do so in the future. The experiences provided have allowed me to learn and transform my consciousness daily. We are One.

I am sincerely blessed and thankful for my wife, daughter, and son for always showing me God's love and for supporting me during my spiritual growth and the writing of this book. Kelly, your patience during my classes, writing and discussions were not unnoticed and very much appreciated. You have challenged me to go deeper within to find the truth. I love each of you unconditionally! My parents, brother, extended family and friends also deserve thanks for the development of this book. We are all part of the Lord's plan for each other to realize our true relationship with God.

I am grateful and thankful for the guidance of Heidi Williams. You have given me the greatest healing and gift possible by helping me discover and unfold my Christ Consciousness from within. Thank you for giving me feedback on this book, plus communing, and contemplating on God's truth during our classes. "For where two or three are gathered together in my name, there am I in the midst of them."—Matthew 18:20.

Introduction

*A*s I sit in the parking lot of the church where I married my beautiful wife, I can't help but wonder in amazement how far I've come since that amazing day fifteen years ago. There I was, a young man taking vows in the name of our Father without truly understanding our relationship with God. I now know this is true among most of us, and surprisingly, this also includes many pastors, priests, metaphysicians, churches or organized religion. They are convinced that they preach the truth, but do they truly know and live the truth. If they did, you would see they are truly set free from fear or error. Unfortunately, this is not the case many times.

This is not a book promoting organized religion. As Mahatma Gandhi said, "God has no religion." Whether you practice Buddhism, Christianity, Paganism, Hinduism, Judaism, Atheism, or any other form of religion does not matter. The goal of this small book is to spread and expand the Christ Consciousness to my family, friends, neighbors, and the world in general.

Although there is no organized religious agenda in this book, I do refer to the Bible for clarifications and examples. I use the word Christ with a different understanding than most do, but that is another topic for another chapter. Please note that I also use the word Father in reference to God in this book. This is not intended to say God is male. I simply use the term, Father, as it was used by the Bible. In reality, God is the Father and Mother to all, the One creative force that the Fifth Commandment tells us to honor. It is my hope that you will begin to understand what the great mystics of the world were really trying to teach.

The concepts that are discussed throughout *Return to Eden* can, and will most likely be, difficult for many to discern. Honestly, the majority of people will not completely grasp the gift of this message. This path is a completely different way than what most have been taught and believe. As the author, I do not take it personally if this book does not resonate with you. It may be foreign and confusing today but can completely resonate with you ten years down the road as your consciousness unfolds. Maybe not. Those that are ready for this message will quickly know that it was meant for your current state of consciousness. Either way, attempt to keep an open mind while reading each chapter.

It is my dream that your spiritual soil will be fertilized so the seed of Truth, Christ or whatever you want to call it can be planted. Then in time, you will know My peace. You may ask yourself, "How can a small book like this accomplish such a fantastic feat?" I asked myself the same question. If I can only reach one, two or three individuals with this book's message, it is meant to be. These few then, in turn, discover the Christ or God within, then they may, in turn, do the same for others in their own way. A great ripple effect will develop, and then together we can truly return to the great Garden of Eden.

Seven Keys to the Mastery of Christ Consciousness

2

Live and demonstrate the fullness of God's Omnipresence. Physical form is not your identity. Your life is the Infinite individuality of Spirit expressing itself. You are this Omnipresence.

Eden Lost

*J*magine being born not as a baby, but a fully grown, mature adult. All of your five senses are developed along with your sixth and seventh senses. You ask, "Sixth and seventh senses?" Yes, we all have these two extra senses, but they have been neglected throughout history and need to be redeveloped and refined. The sixth sense is your intuition, and the seventh sense is what I call the Christ Consciousness. It is your connection with the One power. You may name it God, Father, Lord, Yahweh, Jehovah, Allah, Shiva, Buddha, Krishna, Jesus Christ, etc., it does not matter what the name may be. I digress though, as this is a topic that will be touched upon throughout later chapters and could easily be a book in and of itself.

Let us return to the opening topic with our scenario of experiencing being born fully grown. Although you are an adult, you see and experience everything through the perception of a newborn. Everything has a sense of wonder and is awe-inspiring. It is all beautiful and blissful to take in. You see a newborn fawn, hear the melody of a songbird, feel the gentle breeze, smell the aroma of the nearby flowers and taste the sweetness of wild berries. It is all so pleasing and peaceful.

You also have the same wonder and reactions when you see an ordinary brown rock on the ground or feel the sharpness of a thorn as it pokes you. This amazement is also attained by the action of you yawning. Even silence and stillness are exciting to you. Although to our modern twenty-first century consciousness, these types of experiences seem mundane or painful, the adult newborn you are in our scenario is pleased with having the experience of these items.

Now let us take this a step farther. Remember you are experiencing everything through the perception of a grown newborn. This time you hear the cry of the fawn you saw earlier. As you turn your attention towards the fawn, you see that a large wolf has claimed it for his breakfast. What do you feel? Before you answer that question, remember you are looking through the consciousness of a babe. Do you feel sadness, disgust, pity, or any sense of right or wrong? No. You are in complete awe and wonder of the entire experience. There is absolutely no judgment. It just Is. There are no good, bad, or unfortunate experiences. You have a sense of knowing that It just Is as It is meant to be, and you feel all is well.

This is where your sixth and seventh senses come into your awareness. You have that inner knowing which allows you to realize you are not alone, and you are safe. You hear that inner voice of the Father, or God or whatever you want to name the omnipotent, omniscient and omnipresent life force, guiding, teaching and loving you. There is no judgment, good or bad. Everything just Is. You realize that you are in paradise or the

Garden of Eden. You are just as Adam and Eve initially were, One with everything.

So then, our next question is, "How did Adam and Eve lose themselves from Eden?" We are told of the story of the serpent, the tree of knowledge, the forbidden fruit and the original sin. Can we take this story literally, or is there more meaning to it? I remind you, this is not a book on one organized religion. Each religion has similar stories to Adam and Eve. This story just happens to be the one I was taught.

If we go with the story most were taught at a young age in Western civilizations, we are told God creates Adam out of dust and places him in the Garden of Eden. Adam is instructed to eat freely from all the trees in the garden, but he is not to consume from the tree of knowledge of good and evil. Thereupon, Eve is created from one of Adam's ribs to be his companion. Both are currently innocent and do not bear any shame of their nakedness. Nonetheless, the serpent misleads Eve into eating fruit from the forbidden tree of knowledge, and she presents the fruit to Adam. The act of eating the fruit bestows added knowledge upon them. This knowledge gives them the ability to judge and accept cynical and ruinous concepts such as good versus bad, shame and wickedness. God, in turn, damns the serpent and the ground. The Father or God informs Adam and Eve of the consequences of their sin of disobeying God. Then God banishes Adam and Eve from the Garden of Eden.

What does this story truly mean? Is it a complex or simple concept and lesson to understand? The answer to this second question is yes and no. I will do my best to explain this as we go along on this journey together, but the answer if it is a simple or complex concept to grasp lies in your consciousness. The simple explanation is we are all at different states and levels of consciousness. If you want to break it down to a basic truth, then you could say we are consciousness, period. Depending on the stage of consciousness you are currently living within will determine how simple or complex this concept is. For some of you, it will just "click" and seem like the concept has always been a part of you. It will be as if it was merely unlocked from within your consciousness. For others, it will not "click", and you will most likely quickly lose interest in this book and set aside possibly never picking it up again. If that is the case, then so be it; although I do encourage you to continue reading so you may transform your consciousness to a new level. If this is not the book for you, the book that will "click" for you is out there. Understand this important detail though, a transformed consciousness level of one person does not make that particular person better than another. We are all equal, but we are also on different journeys at this moment in time. Everyone is on a different platform of consciousness. That is why we all perceive our experiences differently. It just is how It is.

Some of you may be struggling to understand the concept of the tree of knowledge of good and evil. You may think, "What is wrong with knowledge? Doesn't knowledge lead you to the truth?" John 8:32 states, "And ye shall know the truth, and the truth shall make you free." Although this phrase is interpreted, used and abused in many ways today, it has become a common Western belief or quote that the truth shall set you free. But is the knowledge you have necessarily the Truth?

You see, the tree of knowledge of good and evil was developed or cultivated in the human mind. It was not literally a tree, but the birth of the human consciousness; a consciousness apart from God. This was the beginning of a new level of consciousness that began to separate Adam and Eve, who represent us, from the creator. Timothy 4:4 tells us, "For every creation of God is good, and nothing that is received with thanksgiving should be rejected." Adam and Eve knew this from the beginning. Everything was as It is. The It is capitalized because It is God. There was One power, and that power was God, the Father or whatever name you have for this power. When you realize there is One power, there is no fear in your experiences. As soon as a second power is developed, in Eden's story it was the development of good versus evil, then fear, stress and all other types of emotions come in to haunt you. This is the birth of self-awareness for Adam and Eve, and it is the destruction of God-awareness. There was no more Oneness between Adam, Eve and God. A duality was formed. This was one of the major lessons Jesus was trying to teach us. John 10:30, "I and the Father are One."

Did the serpent represent the Devil or Satan? Think about this. If all that the Lord created was good, why would a devil be created? If we take the Adam and Eve story literally, it would be safe to assume the serpent or Satan was more cunning than God or Christ the Creator when he tempted Adam and Eve. That cannot be possible because God is omniscient, omnipotent and omnipresent. The serpent represented our ego that convinced us that we could judge better than the Father. It was not another entity that tempted Adam and Eve or even us today. It is our ego that causes this separate consciousness, this belief in two powers and the appearance of error. This was the original sin and to this day is an error we need to alter.

There are many people in the world that have the universal belief of a balance between good and evil. Just the other day, I listened to a metaphysical healer that is on his awakening journey state this very notion. He was adamant that for every good in this world there must be a bad. He stated that humans must just learn how to balance this dual power belief. Is that the solution to finding happiness, peace, and love? That is quite the roller coaster ride that I personally will not partake in. It does not have to be this way, and it was not meant to be this way. This belief is the error as it falls directly into the same trap Adam and Eve self-inflicted upon themselves.

So, it was not God who banished Adam and Eve from the Garden of Eden. It was Adam and Eve themselves that chose the banishment path as they began to disunify their Oneness in the Father. Just as the Prodigal Son, we must awaken ourselves from this illusion of self apart from God and embark on the journey back to our immaculate conception. It is of vital importance that we reprogram this very same error, that most of us demonstrate today, so we may return to Eden. The key to the garden is by ridding ourselves of all labels of good and evil. By doing so, we then can banish all types of error that we experience in our daily living. This will unlock the gate. When we do return to Eden, we will be received by our Father with the statement from Luke 15:13, "Son you are ever with me, and all that I have is yours." We will then be home!

> "Man is always seeking a power, a power to overcome something or destroy something; and therefore, he is not living in the awareness of God, because in the realization of the presence of God there is no need to overcome, to destroy, or to do anything."
>
> —Joel S. Goldsmith

3

*Realize, accept and live the fullness of
Divine Consciousness. Consciousness of
God is consciousness of the individual. There
is One all-embracing consciousness. This
consciousness is ever with you regardless of
what you experience from your five senses.*

The Need for Eden

hy do we need to return to Eden? This question can be answered by analyzing the statement, "The grass is always greener on the other side." This statement is similar to the continuous search for happiness or peace we strive for in human life. We have all been guilty of these thought processes at one time or another. For a lot of us, we fall into this trap, otherwise known as error, and cannot escape the vicious circle of the material world. There can be no doubt that focusing on the material world and your perceived needs divert us from creating a fulfilling and peaceful life. A simple example of this truth is when the well-known comedian of the late twentieth century Richard Pryor stated, "There was a time in my life when I thought I had everything—millions of dollars, mansions, cars, nice clothes, beautiful women and every other materialistic thing you can imagine. Now I struggle for peace."

What is happiness? Is happiness something we can see, hear, smell, taste or feel? Is happiness something you experience? Where can it be found? Is happiness and peace found in the external world, or is happiness found within each of us? Is happiness something that needs to be found, or do we already possess it? These are great questions to contemplate as we explore this topic. Maybe, just maybe, happiness is a state of consciousness.

Now let us look at some of the common ways we look for happiness or peace, or when we error as perceiving the grass is greener on the other side. Think back to your childhood experience because this is where this dangerous pattern begins growing. Actually, it can be said that the cycle started before you were born because of the universal belief in material happiness. There were times you just thought the only way you could be happy was if you had a particular toy. Your parents obliged and bought you the latest and greatest toy you desired, and you were then happy and at peace. The joyful excitement of the toy lasts for a few weeks, sometimes only a few days, and then this delight quickly fades. At this point, another toy catches your attention. Unhappiness and inner conflict begin to develop again as you repeat the process of thinking you need this toy to be fulfilled. The cycle continues to increase through your teenage years with, but not limited to, iPhones, electronics and clothes. Then as an adult, you continue with more clothes, vehicles, real estate, hobby collections, large screen televisions, smartphones, and many other material items. The cycle is so difficult to break. All you end up with is an expansive collection of objects, but still no peace and happiness.

Another common material trap is money, which is the result of desiring more material. Now please don't believe money is bad or evil. We all heard the common saying, "Money is the root of all evil." That is not the message I am attempting to convey, and that again brings us back to Adam and Eve's original sin of believing in good and evil. Money is not evil. Throughout history, society has taken the stance that money is evil. This stance is clearly obvious as it is repeatedly displayed on national media outlets. Money is not the error. The reliance of and lust for money to bring happiness is the error. Timothy 6:10 is the original quote and says, "For the love of money is the root of all evil: which while some coveted after, they have erred from the faith, and pierced themselves through with many sorrows." Money is just one of the many ways God's supply is translated into our experience. God is our consciousness and money coming into our life is one effect of the Lord's presence.

As an adult, you feel that more money will bring happiness, even though we all know the saying, "Money can't buy you happiness." Your rebuttal is, "Yes, but it sure would make things a lot easier." Well, yes and no. It depends on your level of consciousness, intentions, your perceived need and what the money truly means to you. So, you begin your search for more money to attain your peace. This leads to changes in employment, whether it is promotions or complete career changes. Your peace lasts for a while until you realize you perceive the need for more money again, or that the current employment change is causing more stress. The never-ending cycle continues. You have become the hamster on the wheel. Ecclesiastes 5:10 warns us, "Whoever loves money never has enough; whoever loves wealth is never satisfied with their income. This too is meaningless."

Another example of cautionary advice is found in Matthew 6:24, "No one can serve two masters. Either you will hate the one and love the other, or you will be devoted to the one and despise the other. You cannot serve both God and money."

The mindful "ah ha" thought then comes in. You exclaim, "I will find happiness in relationships. That is where happiness and peace is. Who cares what material items, money or career I have? I'll have peace as long as I have someone who loves me. Besides, relationships aren't material." The thought of a relationship isn't material, but the person you are seeking is. You begin another adventure of searching for that peace and happiness. Mr. or Mrs. Right comes along, then they turn into Mr. or Mrs. Wrong. If you're lucky, you find the one for you. Realize though, that every relationship at one time or another can be a source of dispute, disagreement or disharmony. This is true even of a great marriage. Conflicts arise here or there that may be as small as differences of opinions or as large as abuse or divorce. Then there is the ultimate heartbreaker for happily married couples, the universal belief of mortality and physical death of your spouse. There is no guaranteed consistency of your happiness or peace in relationships. This is also true of relationships other than romantic ones. It is all the same reliance on the material, which in this case is people. This is not to say we should avoid relationships. On the contrary, relationships are meant to be enjoyed and cherished. We are meant to experience relationships. The appearance of reliance on the relationship for fulfillment is the error. Psalm 146:3 admonished us of this very topic, "Put not your trust in princes, nor in the son of man, in whom there is no help."

The innumerable pattern of this search repeats itself in countless material items. Think of the many ups and downs we or loved ones have experienced in our search for peace, happiness, and fulfillment in medical treatments, physical health, fitness and exercise, vacations, competitions, sports, and entertainment or any other type of material comfort you can think of. It is the same error no matter what it may be named as long as it is material.

What about finding happiness and peace in organized religion or church? Yes, peace and happiness can be found in organized religion if our Oneness with God is truthfully taught and your consciousness is ready to receive this truth. Many churches have the very best intentions, but in my experience, in Western societies, churches lack the basic understanding of the true teachings of Jesus. John 10:30-36 states, "I and the Father are one... 'We are not stoning You for any good work,' said the Jews, 'but for blasphemy, because You, who are a man, declare Yourself to be God.' Jesus answered them, 'Is it not written in your Law, I have said you are "gods"?" God manifests himself as us, therefore, he is us. We all are the Holy Trinity once our consciousness rises to the truth. We are the Father, which is our spirit or soul. God is the spirit, the soul and the life of all being. We are the Son, which is our body manifested by the Christ

Consciousness. The body is the temple of the living God. We are the Holy Spirit, which is our consciousness or mind. The mind is the instrument through which God functions. These truths have been twisted or misinterpreted by many.

Many go to church hoping to be set free by the truth; to find happiness and peace through a relationship with God. Again, some do find this, but most do not. Instead, many times we are misled by being taught fear and a God apart from us. We are taught that God is vengeful by punishing or rewarding you depending on your sins or lack of sins. Power is given to Satan and our errors. Fear is the teaching tool of choice. The church leads us to believe God is somewhere out there, and the only place we can find God is at church or with their particular religion. A reliance on the church is manifested, and the belief we must look outward instead of inward for the Lord. We end up leaving Church feeling uplifted many times and pat ourselves on the back, but this is short lived as we quickly come down and yearn for that peace once again. The error is in relying on the church or organized religion as it is run by "mortal man." We fall into the same trap as the relationship error discussed above.

People cannot find a sustaining happiness, joy, peace or fulfillment in the reliance of the material world. The path to what you desire begins with the truth. As Mary Baker Eddy stated over a century ago, "Truth is immortal, error is mortal." The degree of acknowledgment we profess towards the two powers of good and evil governs the peace of our true being.

There is only One power, and it resides within us. We all have the ability to release this One without earthly materialistic dependencies. Go within yourself!

> " Stop looking outside for scraps of pleasure or fulfillment, for validation, security, or love—you have a treasure within that is infinitely greater than anything the world can offer. "
>
> —Eckhart Tolle

Seven Keys to the Mastery of Christ Consciousness

4

*Realize, accept and live the fullness of
Divine Love. Divine Love individualizes,
expressing as individual love. There is never
a time while in your Spiritual Identity that
you are not in the Love of the Father.*

The Key to Eden

*U*nderstanding that authentic peace and happiness cannot be found in the material world is an initial step in returning to Eden. What is this "peace" that will lead to fulfillment? Where can we find it? Jesus gave us a tremendous clue when he said, "Peace I leave with you, My peace I give unto you: not as the world giveth, give I unto you. Let not your heart be troubled, neither let it be afraid." Do you see the clue? "My peace I give unto you: not as the world giveth..." Jesus was not telling us that he wanted us to have the peace bestowed upon us that was created by the human man Jesus; instead, he was telling us to have the peace of God that comes from within us.

Many times, throughout history great masters of Christ or God Consciousness have used the words "I" and "My" in their teachings. You will see these examples demonstrated in the words of Jesus, Buddha, Lao Tzu, Paul, John, Peter, and numerous others. These masters understood and lived the truth in their consciousness, that we are all One with God. Don't be fooled into thinking they meant they are literally God and no one else is One with God. The masters knew that we are all One because we all come from the Father. The words "I" and "My"

29

are describing their oneness with the Lord, the creative force of all. Romans 8:17 explains, "And if children, then heirs; heirs of God, and joint-heirs with Christ…" The consciousness of the masters reached such an ascended level that they were truly one with the Father. This truth showed through them at a stage of consciousness that most cannot grasp. They demonstrated their Oneness with God even in their speech.

If any of us attaining the Christ Consciousness would say, "I stand on holy ground.", what would that mean? It would simply mean that wherever I stand is holy because God is One with me. The Father is wherever I stand because I have attained a Oneness with the Lord that is built upon God's truth. This truth can be demonstrated by any of us as long as we rise in consciousness. This rising in consciousness is the immaculate conception. It is the miraculous birth of a new you. The old material sense of you is crucified, and you are born anew in the Christ or God Consciousness. This is a tremendous internal battle that we will have in releasing from within and reaching this conscious platform. We must shed the error of the universal beliefs we have been taught or exposed to since birth. This is not an easy feat as you may find yourself questioning every-thing, and you may feel lost at times. This questioning is the start of something special, a true relationship with God. Will all of us continue on this path and find our way to Christ? Matthew 7:14 tells us, "Because strait is the gate, and narrow is the way, which leadeth unto life, and few there be that find it." John explains this entire process of consciousness unfolding in the book of Revelation. This story is very cryptic and full of symbolism. Therefore, it has been greatly misinterpreted by many. The entire story is the inner unfoldment of the Christ in human consciousness. It describes an internal battle, not a literal external battle. The best interpretation of this story I have come across was in Marchette Chute's book *The End of the Search*.

The Bible is a written record of humankind's experiences in raising the consciousness of our true relationship with God throughout history. Is the Bible something that happened in the past or is it happening for each of us at this very moment? Scripture is currently unfolding in each one of us. Your consciousness is the Bible. Every experience in the Bible, every character, is already within your consciousness. Each story can be used as an analogy for our personal development of God Consciousness. Since we are all at different levels of consciousness, we are all currently living different stories or experiences of the Bible. The examples in the Bible have no value until you consciously realize their relationship to your current state of consciousness.

Throughout history, many have spent much time, contemplation, debate, and energy on either finding or theorizing the whereabouts, the form or power of the Holy Grail. People have searched far and wide when all they needed to do was look within. That's right, that Oneness with the Father that is found within you is the Holy Grail. Jesus said to Philip in John 14:10, "Believest thou not that I am in the Father, and the Father in me? the words that I speak unto you I speak not of myself: but the Father that dwelleth in me, he doeth the works." Again, we are

One with God. The Lord is our life force and only power. If God is omnipresent, and we are One with God, then we, in turn, are immortal. God's objective is not for us to remain in one particular human form on earth perpetually, more so than it is for us to stay a baby, a child, a teenager or stay a middle age adult forever. We truly are living an endless life. The essence of us, which is God, is immortal. This essence does not become an elderly body. We are always the body of true maturity. Our souls then transform by traveling out of our manifested bodies into the next chapter of our being, in which yet the perpetuation of our service on the earth plane may continue. The holy grail has always been hidden in plain sight. One could say that we are the holy grail.

We are not material beings; we are spiritual beings. We are spiritual souls or spirits that live One with God eternally. The Father manifests himself as us; therefore, he is us, and we are One with him. If God is omnipresent, omniscient and omnipotent, and he lives within us, then the same can be said of us. God is the spirit, the great Invisible. We can never escape from the presence of God. We are not two; we are an inseparable One. Embrace this truth and be One with God! As you do this, fear will fade from different aspects of your life. If you think about it, fear is really atheism. Fear is the belief in multiple powers, and unbeknownst to you, secretly enables the stance that there is no God. That stance activates the continuous appearance of the fear cycle, the error that haunts so many on a daily basis.

The best way to understand the truth of our Oneness with God is to be still. We must learn that God's power, the One power, is manifested in stillness and silence. Sit in stillness and contemplate God's grace. It is one thing to read scriptures and quotes, but they will not reveal their truth to you unless you contemplate them in stillness and silence. Some call this meditation, I simply like to call it stillness. "Be still and know that I am God: I will be exalted among the heathen, I will be exalted in the earth.", Psalm 46:10. Don't just read this scripture like an affirmation. Sit in stillness and contemplate or meditate on this verse. It is only in stillness and in silence that the truth will come to you. Always seek inner guidance in everything, no matter how great you are at something. It is a way of life that takes practice and discipline.

This does not mean we sit around all day meditating. Yes, we are in this world but not of this world; but we still have responsibilities to tend. We are meant to experience and learn. Take an active role in the life you have chosen to create. God created us to act with his guidance and Oneness. It is not a lazy way of living. You and I cannot just sit back and let God do everything for us. If you take this route, you lose your Oneness with the Father. You would be separate from God and relying on a God out there apart from yourself. This is not the truth. This is an error in the belief of two powers. There is only One.

This book is what I would consider an introduction to the way of living as One with God. I am by no means the absolute authority on this wonderful gift. The authority comes from the Father within just as the great masters of the past and present, who attained this authority by truly living as One with God.

This book is being written in the midst of my immaculate conception and development of the Christ Consciousness. My journey is not complete and may never be complete in this lifetime, but does that mean I should just abandon this gift because I may not attain it one hundred percent? Absolutely not! I bear witness to the love of God that has been manifested in my life from within on a daily basis. This presence is the ultimate healing power as it is the only true power. Swami Vivekananda captured this when he said, "Love of God increases every moment and is ever new, to be known only by feeling it... We need no demonstration, no proof... So long as you hold yourself separated by a hair's breadth from this Eternal One, fear cannot go...He who follows the God of Truth with devotion, to him the God of Truth reveals himself... It is impossible for us to find God outside of ourselves." In an upcoming chapter, I will list greater references and authorities for the further development of the gift of Christ or God Consciousness. So, if you are serious about doing the work needed, please do not stop at this book. You will discover that you will be guided to what you need to fulfill this journey. The objective of living a spiritual life is to awaken in God's image and likeness as stated in Genesis. Then you realize your true spiritual being as Christ, the Son of God.

We must accept that there is One power. There is no existing good or evil in anyone or anything. Matthew 19:17 tells us of Jesus stating this truth, "And he said unto him, Why callest thou me good? there is none good but one, that is, God:

but if thou wilt enter into life, keep the commandments." We must acknowledge that the Lord is solely good. When we see good in the world, it is not you or me doing the good. It is God's good manifesting itself through us. If the appearance of bad or evil shows forth, realize it is just that, an appearance or suggestion. It is an error of the human mind. This appearance of error is an illusion manifested by our ego and has no power over us. When we attain this level of consciousness, we will be amazed at the forms of supply and good fortune that manifests in our lives. We will then find "My peace," the ultimate peace of God. Be cautioned though, you do not take this path to gain supply and good fortune. You take this path to Eden to experience a true relationship and Oneness with God. The supply and good fortune are only by-products of God's presence within you and in everything around you.

The moment you accept the false perception of good or evil, you are outside of the Garden of Eden. This is a belief in a second power we call error. All error is a deceptive appearance. It is an intellectual misinterpretation that does not truly exist. The source of all problems is the universal belief in two powers. We are born into the consciousness of universal beliefs. It is like being sentenced to a form of prison at birth. The only way to liberate yourself from prison is to remove the ego's judgment of good or evil. Do not form a reliance on the material perception of our being, rely on your spiritual sense where truth is found. All error should be impersonalized. Realize it is not the individual person causing the error. Instead, it is the universal belief's trance we have been living in that is causing the error, not the individual being. Do not try to correct the error. Instead, solely focus on the truth, not the appearance or suggestion of error. See people as they truly are, the fathomless spirit or soul of God.

> "Not my will but Yours, Father, be done in me and through me. Let me always be a channel of blessings, today, now, to those that I contact, in every way. Let my going in, my coming out be in accord with that You would have me do, and as the call comes, 'Here I am, send me, use me!'"

—Edgar Cayce

Traveling Down the Path

*T*raveling the spiritual path back to Eden first requires an understanding of God's truth. Most of us will find that we cannot jump directly into contemplative meditation without having the basic comprehension of the ancient mystical principles that the masters taught throughout history. This conception of truth is the cornerstone to obtaining your rightful place in the Garden of Eden. The study of the truth is crucial for ensuring your spiritual soil is fertile before the seed of the Father's truth can take root and become manifested in your daily living. If you attempt to plant a seed into the infertile soil, the seed will quickly wither away. The same can be said if you attempt to discern your Oneness with God without first fertilizing your consciousness with the mystical truth of the Lord. Your journey to Eden would abruptly end in a marvelous bewilderment.

An alternative way to describe this process is using the story of Noah's Ark as an analogy. Many religions from around the world have their own version of this parable. Understand this is a very condensed and basic version of the story, as most of us already know it. The world was foul with wickedness, which causes God the desire to destroy the people, animals, birds and creeping things. Because of Noah's righteousness, God establishes His covenant with Noah and instructs him to build an ark in which his family may enter. God then instructs Noah to take seven pairs of all animals onto the boat. The great flood engulfed the earth and everything living on land perished. The flood subsides as the ark lands on the mountains of Ararat, and Noah's family and the animals repopulate the earth. God then promises never to flood the earth again.

Now let us see how this story can relate to our concept we discussed in the opening paragraph of this chapter. Instead of the world being foul with wickedness, it is Noah's consciousness that is polluted with the error or universal belief of more than One power, otherwise known as good and evil, that has been fantasized into his mind since birth. A spiritual spark was then ignited in Noah's consciousness that started him on the path of truth and Oneness with God. At this time, Noah begins to build the cornerstone of truth into his consciousness to prepare himself for the flood of truth that God, from within, was soon bestowing upon him.

After Noah's foundation of truth, or ark, is built and populated with God's "creatures of truth", Noah is then prepared for the great flood of truth. The number of pairs of creatures was seven each. In ancient Judaism, the number seven represented the blessing of completeness and holiness. The seven pairs of creatures could very well represent the blessings of the wholeness of Christ Consciousness that poured into his consciousness. Noah unraveled the Lord's truth within his consciousness to complete his Oneness with God. The flood of truth comes into Noah's consciousness destroying all of his man-made universal beliefs. This is a very tumultuous and arduous time for Noah. This is symbolized by the torrential storms during the flood. Can you contemplate how difficult it is to realize so much of what you have been taught in life is an error? It is a large pill to swallow indeed. Perhaps you are realizing this difficulty at this very moment. Do not give up though, as the realization of your true divine self is worth any material world sacrifice you may need to experience.

You may ask, "What about his family? What do they represent?" As a person transforms his or her consciousness to the truth of God, it is natural for this consciousness to grow in others that are close to them. Noah's consciousness enabled his family to also rise and transform their consciousness to one degree or another during this entire process. This is symbolized by Noah's family being sufficiently capable of entering the ark, otherwise known as his foundation of truth, permitting them to continue on the journey with him. Understand though, that his family needed a base consciousness that allowed the seed of truth to be planted. Their conscious soil was fertile ground. If a person's consciousness is not ready for the truth, he or she will not understand it, and therefore, will not voyage with Noah. Noah's family also represented the companionship that we need in this transformation of consciousness. It is truly a difficult path to voyage by yourself, but the journey can be easier with the company of others with harmonious awareness.

As the flood of truth starts to subside, Noah begins to make sense of his revelation and experiences a rising consciousness. At last, his consciousness is full of God's truth, and the flood of truth ends. The mountains of Ararat could represent the highest point of consciousness attained, in which no error or universal belief could touch. At this point, all of the errors of ego have been washed away. Noah will never again experience the flood of truth from God, as he is born anew and can never return to his old consciousness or "the wicked world." His Christ or God Consciousness begins to spread across the world developing fertile land in others' conscious minds to plant the seeds of God's truth.

This is exactly what we must execute while starting this wonderful path to the Garden of Eden. We must flood our consciousness with the Father's truth. As we do this, all errors of our ego begin to be cleansed from our consciousness. This, in time, leads us to illumination, and we become a living demonstration of God's presence. A basic blueprint for this journey is first to study the written truth to attain its correct comprehension; experience the spirit of truth through contemplating the written truth in stillness, and to surround yourself with like-minded students or teachers of truth for assistance during this spiritual unfoldment. My hope is to fill your "toolbox" of truth with enough tools so as to make your journey to Eden as resolute as possible.

One of the easiest tools of truth to utilize comes in the form of books. I will suggest various authors that can help you unravel or clarify the truth during your return to Eden, but ultimately, you must find the authors or books that resonate with you. A particular author may have cultivated my consciousness but may not be what your level of consciousness needs. You will pleasantly discover though, that your consciousness will attract the perfect books for you as you go on this spiritual journey. Understand that this is only the first step. A book can open the door to higher consciousness, but the completeness of Christ Consciousness ultimately involves you going within for answers or truth, not looking outward to find the truth.

I will begin with the author that had the biggest influence on my consciousness. This was Joel S. Goldsmith. I was already in the midst of my spiritual unfoldment at the time my spiritual teacher introduced me to one of Joel's book "The Heart of Mysticism." Once I started reading this book, I could not put it down. It was like my own consciousness wrote it and was speaking the truth to me. Joel spread truth through The Infinite Way. This was the name Joel gave to his spiritual teaching. He offered many different books that can expand your consciousness of spiritual truth into such a deep understanding. Although his message was similar in many of his books, the variety of methods used to describe his principles enabled the unfolding of my consciousness through many of his books. It is my belief that you cannot go wrong with any of his written or recorded works.

There are many spiritual truth authors and books throughout history. In our western society, the Bible is considered the greatest. All of the Father's truths are found in the Bible. The stumbling block is that it can be strenuous to comprehend at times and is often misinterpreted. Stories cannot always be taken literally, as they were often times cryptic and full of symbolism. Another issue is many people simply quote scripture as though they are affirmations without looking within for the true meaning. One must sit in stillness and contemplate what scripture is truly revealing to us. This contemplation can swiftly and forcefully bring about the truth at times like a lightning strike, but there are other times when the contemplation takes months before spiritual truth reveals itself to you. The key to understanding the Bible is stillness and silence. Go within and let God's grace, love, and wisdom come to you at God's will, not your ego's will.

If the Bible or Joel S. Goldsmith is not for you, then look elsewhere. Many of the following authors offer a variety of methods and writing styles for flooding your consciousness with the truth. There is no particular order or bias to these authors. Each serves the Father's purpose in his or her own unique way while displaying the veracity of being One with God. Find the author or book that speaks to your spirit within. A substantial list of spiritual authors includes, but is not limited to Henry T. Hamblin, Walter Lanyon, Mary Baker Eddy, Eric Butterworth, Marchette Chute, Barbara Mary Muhl, Herb Fitch, Virginia Stephenson, Lillian DeWaters, Eckhart Tolle, Charles Filmore, Mooji, Bill Skiles and Murdo MacDonald-Bayne.

Another tool that can be utilized is communion with spiritual teachers. This is exactly what Jesus was as he shared private spiritual introspections to his disciples. He was the master teacher of God's living truth. Using teachers for spiritual growth and transforming your consciousness can have vast benefits, or it can possibly be detrimental to some degree. The requisite is the same as everything on this path to Eden; go within to find your answer, or in this case, your teacher. There are times, as it happened to me, that your teacher is revealed to you, and you absolutely know they are the correct teacher for your particular level of consciousness at that moment. Then there are times that you allow your mind to tell you differently than your inner wisdom. Your mind may tell you an excuse like, this teacher is too far of a drive for me, or my friend really likes this other teacher. Even though your highest self informs you he or she was the correct teacher for you, you betray the guidance and allow your mind to tell you a different story. Once again, this may cause a cease of conscious unfoldment and stop your journey dead in its tracks. I cannot state this enough, no matter what you do, go within! You already have all of the answers you need within you as you embrace being One with the Creator.

While taking on the role of student with a spiritual teacher, there are a few components of this relationship you need to keep in mind. First and foremost, if you listened to your inner self when choosing a teacher, realize that God is working through the teacher for your spiritual unfoldment. There is no power of the teacher separate from God as long as the teacher has spiritual integrity. Your teacher is a form of God's supply. God is revealed through this Oneness.

The thought may arise of, "What is spiritual integrity?" This basically means the teacher has strong spiritual principles. This person not only teaches the truth, he or she also abides in and lives the truth. Just as Jesus showed the way, he not only spoke the truth but was a living example of the truth. As you travel along this path to Eden, you further develop your intuitive and spiritual senses as your consciousness ascends. You will intuitively feel if you and your teacher are in alignment or not. A major warning that the teacher is not fruitful for your development is when you witness ego in action. There is a fine line at times where well-intended teachers cross over and allow their ego to enter their teachings. As we know, ego is what caused the error that dismissed us from the Garden of Eden in the first place. You will observe contradictions between the teachings and actions of the teacher. If this were to happen, it is time to move on. Staying in this type of student-teacher relationship will only promote confusion and internal discordance.

A student must also be cognizant of their attachment to the teacher. For some, there may be the potential to be so enamored with their teacher to the degree the student develops a reliance on the teacher. The teacher is put on a pedestal, while the student feels they need the teacher to accomplish any spiritual growth or healing. This action shows the fact that the student is not truly understanding the truth and their conscious ascension has stalled. You must stay on the path to Eden by remembering the Kingdom of God is your consciousness. You have the answers within you and do not need to rely on your teacher to bring them to fruition. Be One with the Lord and go within. Also, realize no matter how extraordinary your teacher may be, there will come a time when you must part ways as your heightened consciousness will either stand confidently on its own, or you will need another teacher to expand your consciousness in new ways.

Teachers also have to stay aware of the possibility of student reliance. If this were to happen, the teacher should take the example of Jesus. Jesus says in John 16:7, "Nevertheless I tell you the truth; It is expedient for you that I go away: for if I go not away, the Comforter will not come unto you; but if I depart, I will send him unto you." A teacher absent of ego will do this exact action while knowing, abiding and living the truth of God Consciousness. A teacher with ego as his or her true guide will encourage and feed the student's reliance on the teacher.

As a student, you must discern the only individual that can ultimately deliver you to Eden is you. Flood your consciousness with truth, but don't rely on books or teachers to transform your consciousness for you. You must do the work! As stated before, this is not a lazy way of life. It takes discipline and commitment as the road to Eden is straight and narrow. Develop the reliance on the Father within, not on books, classes or teachers. Realize your rightful place as heir to God, for the Father is the soul of man. Go forth and be One with God.

"The Light of one human being who discovers the Truth has been lighting human existence for thousands of years. Such is the power of a human being who realizes the Truth of who they are."

—Mooji

Living in Eden

*T*he underlying message or purpose of this book is to change your consciousness from a material perception of one's life to the spiritual reality of one's life. Live your true divinity. Move away from the material awareness that, in many cases, organized religion bestows upon us. The error that is taught many times is that God is found out there somewhere or can only be found at Church. Alternatively, find within yourself, not somewhere outside in the material world, the spiritual consciousness that you are One with God. Free yourself from the many forms of material supply and have spiritual consciousness be your supply. It is best to discern that material items are not truly your supply. The grace, love, and wisdom of God within you is your true supply, and the material items are just the effect of this supply. Do not give power to the mortal or human perception of the world by accepting the appearances or suggestions of good and evil.

We must embrace and live the spiritual life as we live in the Garden of Eden. Those of us on this path have awakened from our material world slumber and are conscious that each one of us is truly One with God. God created us in his image and likeness. Romans 8:17 informs us of this, "And if children, then heirs; heirs of God, and joint-heirs with Christ; if so be that we suffer with him, that we may be also glorified together." Our goal for consciousness is to become fully aware of our true spiritual identity as Christ, the Son of God, or whatever name you would like to give this realization.

We are the Holy Trinity when we are One with God. God manifests as us. If God manifests as us, then God is us. In turn, if God is us, we are One. Our spirit or soul is the Father, the life of everything. Our body is the Son, the temple of God or of our soul. The consciousness of our mind is where the Holy Spirit functions. This is also the place where the immaculate conception takes place. This immaculate conception is the process of the Holy Spirit or Christ Consciousness descending upon you. It is the point where your consciousness has that "click" with the realization of who you truly are. You are more than the human form and name you were given at birth. You are the sum total of our being, the spirit, body, and consciousness, and this entirety of our being is God.

Going within or meditation is the essential daily activity needed for continued realization of our true identities as heirs of the Father. It is not the meditation most think of like chanting, humming, or making affirmations. This type of meditation involves sitting in stillness and silence. We all must have a daily inner communion with God. While you do this, you enter the empty place of the mind that has no thought. Resist attempts of your ego to make judgments like, "this stillness is dull or boring." Once you accept judgments such as those, your ego will begin to manifest other material thoughts taking you from your stillness and, in turn, from God. One does not need to have sensational visions while sitting in stillness or meditation. All you need to do is welcome the emptiness and listen for God or spirit to give you messages. Do not worry if you receive no messages, just enjoy the stillness. God is omniscient; thus, God knows what you need before your human mind knows. You may not need any message at that particular time. If you do receive a message, it is by God's will, not your will. All you need to do is enjoy "My peace" that comes in the stillness. I am positive that you will learn to love this stillness as your ego fades away.

Some of us have "chatter brains" or "monkey minds." This means you may have trouble quieting your mind into stillness. A strategy to remedy this is, to begin with, a period of contemplation of such things as scripture or other quotes of truth from spiritual books or teachers. This can be beneficial even if you do not have constant ego chatter. An example would be to contemplate what does it mean to be "in this world, but not of this world." If your mind veers off track, just release the thought and return to the topic of your contemplation. This process will eventually lead to stillness and silence where ego is absent. At this point, you are communing with God in stillness.

A stumbling block in which many people experience with meditation or prayer is seeking something from the material world. When you partake in meditation or prayer, you must make sure you are not searching for any type of material supply.

Think of the many types of material supply that we search in for happiness. These were discussed in chapter two. This can include simply asking for health in some shape or form. This is asking for some type of material manifestation from God. Remember, God already knows what you need because the Lord is omniscient. This is praying or meditating amiss. Praying or meditating in this manner is acknowledging a second power other than God. You are acknowledging that your ego has a better knowledge of your needs than God. This is the slippery slope that will quickly take you out of the Garden of Eden. At the time you stop searching with your prayers for material supply, you will then be blessed with God's supply. This is when God's grace, love, and wisdom become your sufficiency. Do not attempt to find a material supply for sufficiency. If you pray for something, pray or meditate for God's grace, wisdom or illumination.

What about praying for victory in a conflict or war? Should we pray for this? This is witnessed in the media and at times in churches. Humans constantly ask for victory over other religions, nationalities, races, socioeconomic groups and many other areas. Again, this is praying awry. We are all heirs to the Father. God grants his grace on everyone. God does not favor one over another. We must pray for our enemies; pray for their illumination to God's truth and the birth of their Christ or Spiritual Consciousness. Matthew 5:44 states this perfectly, "But I say unto you, Love your enemies, bless them that curse you, do good to them that hate you, and pray for them which despitefully use you, and persecute you;".

Meditation in stillness helps transform our consciousness from the material world ruled by the ego to the Christ or God Consciousness that brings "My peace" and delivers us into the world of Eden. We are all in this material world, but not of it. We are spiritual beings of God. "God is a Spirit: and they that worship him must worship him in spirit and in truth.", John 4:24. Worshiping in the material sense is not worshiping with God. Practice worshiping by bearing witness to the spiritual presence of God.

We all must practice bearing witness to God's presence daily. A perfect place to begin this communion with God is upon awakening in the morning. As you wake, before you get out of bed, focus on some sort of spiritual truth. It could be as simple as, "God manifests as us, therefore, God is us. If God is us, then I am One with God. I, by myself do not accomplish any good feats, it is the Christ within me that graces me with the love and wisdom to do so. I can accomplish anything with Christ. God, not by my will, but your will, guide me today allowing me to grace others with the Christ Consciousness. We are One."

Follow up this by practicing God's presence throughout the day. At meals acknowledge that God's grace has manifested as your meal and as companionship with family or friends during this meal. Communion with God can happen anywhere. It can be while you are driving your car, or during small breaks throughout the day. This process does not need to be lengthy. Just close your eyes and go within. Obviously, I am not telling you to close your eyes while driving. There will come a point when you will not need to close your eyes to go within. A minute or two of going within is sufficient. Eventually, the length of time in communion will naturally lengthen. You may start with practicing God's presence three times per day, then move up to five, ten, twenty or more times per day. Even when perceived difficult problems emerge throughout the day, you must commune with God. Remember this difficulty you encounter is just a suggestion of a problem, which is truly an error and does not have any power. Christ is within each of us and is omnipotent, omniscient and omnipresent. There is no other power but God, therefore this appearance of error has no power over us and does not truly exist in reality.

A final communion with the Father should take place before you retire for the night. Again, this can take the form of contemplation of God's truth or meditate in stillness and silence. This sets up your consciousness for communing with God even as you sleep. A simple example could be being grateful for the events of the day that God's grace was present. Another method is to simply follow the example of 1 Samuel 3:9, "Therefore Eli said unto Samuel, Go, lie down: and it shall be, if he call thee, that thou shalt say, Speak, LORD; for thy servant heareth. So Samuel went and lay down in his place." In other words, "Commune with me Lord before and as I sleep, for I will listen with my true inner hearing."

The entirety of practicing the Father's presence will lead to such a fantastic unraveling of God Consciousness in your mind. You will build the promise of truly being One with God.

Realization of what the poet Alfred Tennyson said comes into your consciousness, "Closer is He than breathing, and nearer than hands and feet." Despite any prevailing circumstances that may arise, you can swiftly realize your inner stillness and silence and find peace in the Garden of Eden. You always know that wherever you stand is Holy ground, because God is always within you as you are One with God.

As you stand on your Holy ground in Eden, you may feel the urge to start telling everyone you know or meet about your wonderful communions with the God within. Do not do this. This is a sacred relationship that is between you and the Lord. There is a level of secrecy that is needed during the attainment of Christ Consciousness. The only time you should divulge sacred information is when you come across someone that is consciously ready for the truth. Otherwise, allow your relationship as One with God to be sanctified. The act of leading others to Eden will be expounded in another following chapter. This secrecy is especially needed if you are new to this journey to Eden and truly being One with God. Those that cannot yet understand this truth will allow their ego to ridicule you in an attempt to keep you in the material world. This is a much easier task for the ego to accomplish when you are new to the path, then when you have already flooded your consciousness with God's truth.

While in Eden, we are not done expanding our consciousness. We are continuous students of the truth, and therefore, need to be wary of material influences on your consciousness. Yes, it is true that you have beat down your ego and the error of power it once had on you, but it has not been completely taken out of you. There is always the possibility that the ego will try to rise again at times, therefore it is best to avoid television shows and media. These items, including social media, are constant promotions of the belief of good and evil. Their message contradicts the truth and can cause conflict and restriction on your journey to be One with the Father in the Garden of Eden. Mahatma Gandhi gifted us with this advice which can easily pertain to material propaganda, "An error does not become truth by reason of multiplied propagation, nor does truth become error because nobody sees it,"

A phenomenon that may happen as you live in Christ Consciousness is losing interest in previously enjoyed entertainment or hobbies. This is very common as you leave the material world and enter the spiritual world. Many objects or experiences that you once cherished and found enjoyable will start to seem meaningless or empty. That football game or reality show you once loved, will soon disappear from your radar. You may end up letting go of treasured collections and belongings. The yearning for competition may subside or cease to exist. All of the material items you thought could possibly bring you happiness fade away. This can also include some relationships. It is natural to have expiration dates on certain relationships as your consciousness unfolds. The church is another item that may fall by the wayside. You may find yourself listening to a sermon from your pastor and realizing the error in his or her message. The ego of your pastor that you never noticed before suddenly appears front and center. You now see and hear everything with your true sight and hearing, the intuitive and spiritual senses that have been refined as you acknowledged your wholeness with God. The feeling of reliance on the church to find God dissipates, as you know and live the truth of being One with the Father.

As you continue to inhabit Eden, be wary of temptations. Yes, temptations will naturally arise even at a higher consciousness level. There is the possibility of sins to appear. Sinning is basically violating our soul or our spiritual identity as Son of God. You have beaten your ego, but you have not totally removed your ego from your mind. There will be times when the ego sees an opportunity to rise up again and make its presence known. The beauty of your current consciousness is that you can quickly admonish your ego, and it will quickly bow down to your Oneness with the Lord. Do not batter yourself when this happens. Even Jesus had these temptations in the wilderness. The devil, or his ego, pursued Jesus to tempt him into sinning by acknowledging the error of more than one power. "Jesus said to him, "Away from me, Satan! For it is written: 'Worship the Lord your God, and serve him only.", Matthew 4:10. So do not fret if temptations should arise, for all you need to do is bring your thoughts back to God's omnipotence just as Jesus realized. Continue to go forth living your life as the Good Shepherd in the Garden of Eden.

"To the mind that is still, the whole universe surrenders."

—Lao Tzu

Seven Keys to the Mastery of Christ Consciousness

5

Realize, accept and live the fullness of God's Omnipotence. God transfers dominion over the material universe, which is Divine Power, to the Christ of you so that all dominion is in the Father and the Son. Rest in Christ while overcoming the world. Omnipotence rests in your true identity and doesn't need to be invoked or attained. It is what you are in yourself.

Spiritual Health

A major item of the material world that many are concerned with is health and wellness. I have been personally and professionally guilty of this worry for many years as a person in general and as a teacher. In the twentieth century, and still today, the main focus was, or still is, physical health and wellness. We are unceasing in striving to see what the next ultimate fitness routine, nutrition fad, magic health supplement or medication can do for our physical fitness and body image. People jump from one material concept of physical health to another, only to find out happiness cannot be found this way. It is true that we are to take care of our body, the temple of God. 1 Corinthians 6:19-20 informs us of this duty, "Or do you not know that your body is a temple of the Holy Spirit within you, whom you have from God? You are not your own, for you were bought with a price. So glorify God in your body." Yes, exercise and fitness can help with stress and in many other ways, but does it truly give you happiness and health? Exercise and fitness should not be neglected, but this alone will not complete you. 1 Timothy 4:8 states, "For while bodily training is of some value, godliness is of value in every way, as it holds promise for the present life and also for the life to come." I have witnessed many physically fit and so-called healthy people who were not happy or still fell victim to illness and other errors. We spend much energy and money on this vicious material cycle of physical health only to get to the place where we ask ourselves, "What is the point? Why do I keep doing all of this, because I am still not happy, and I still come down with illnesses?"

Then we have the great shift to the concern of mental and emotional health that has rapidly expanded since the turn of our current century. More than ever, people are trying to find a way to combat depression and suicides. We see so many without peace, always searching, and they cannot figure it out. Doctors, psychiatrists, researchers and pharmaceutical companies attempting their best to heal others of their mental and emotional pain. Medications and treatments are developed in vain as this epidemic grows. We start to discern the feeling that no one has it all figured out, not even the top medical professionals; and we would be accurate in our suspicion.

Where do we turn? Spiritual health, that is where we must focus. What is spiritual health? It is everything we have discussed in this book thus far. We need to remove the disconnect between physical, mental, emotional and spiritual health. Spiritual health leads to the fulfillment of all types of health, specifically, mental, emotional and physical wellness. "I can do all things through Christ which strengthens me."—Philippians 4:13. Without spiritual health, we will not reach our wholeness as One with God; therefore, our physical, mental and emotional health can greatly suffer. As we return to Eden, we rid ourselves of the many universal beliefs that have hypnotized us since birth. Acknowledging these universal beliefs, such as we are doomed because of poor heredity, is in direct conflict with God's omnipotence. This is the belief of good and evil that bans us from the Garden of Eden. When a person is a victim of universal beliefs, the person is unaware of how to release themselves from their constraint. We need to understand we are the Law of God because we are rightful heirs of God. Understanding this ensures you carry your own ambiance or aura separate from universal beliefs. We live in the atmosphere of the Father, not the material world.

As you develop a Oneness with God or spiritual health, you become fully aware that you are in control of your body and, in turn, your health. Your body does not influence life, because God is life. How can a material body influence God, the only power? We do not have a life of human separate from God. There is nothing to enhance or lengthen while living as One with our Father. All we need to do is presently witness the life of God as his heirs.

Let us examine the universal belief that we cannot escape heredity that has been passed down throughout our family's generations. Again, God is the only life force; there is no other. "The Spirit Himself testifies with our spirit that we are God's children. And if we are children, then heirs, heirs of God and fellow heirs with Christ," Romans 8:16-17. Yes, our parents are the material implements in which we are born into this world, but who is our true father or creator? Your human parents or God? The answer lies in you knowing that your true identity is spiritual, not material as in your human body. The invisible life force of God created us, hence the heredity of our material human parents is inconsequential. Heredity has no power. Only God is omnipotent.

So again, we return to the original sin of Adam and Eve. Will you let the Tree of Knowledge of good and evil dismiss you from Eden? Will you let your ego, the serpent, tempt you with material powers and universal beliefs? No! You will realize that our soul, not the ego is the author of our health and wellness. The ego is the great deceiver and attempts to make you believe many errors. Ego has no power. There is only One that is omnipotent, and those of us that attain the Christ Consciousness is the One, the Son of God.

I cannot help but reflect on my own life as I write this. It amazes me how clear I can see now from the vantage point of a consciousness in transition. I say my consciousness is in transition at this moment because I know there is an infinite amount more to unravel within. While I was a young child and into my teenage years, I rarely, if ever, got sick. If I did get sick, my illness was short lived. I primarily attribute this lack of illness and general overall wellness to the state of consciousness I had at that time of my life. Although I had no words to describe the workings of my consciousness, I always knew that I had nothing to fear. That still small voice guided and comforted me during those years. For the most part, fear and worry did not exist in me at that time. I did not understand it was the Father within, but I just had a knowing. Nothing troubled me even when situations appeared difficult. An additional reason for my lack of illness was the lack or absence of universal health beliefs being sowed into my consciousness during those early years of this lifetime. I was blessed to have such loving parents that were always there for me. Never was illness and sickness given power by saying such things as, "Stay away from your friend because he has a cold. If you catch his cold germs, you will also get sick." No, I did not hear this. We would play alongside each other no matter who was ill at the moment with no worries of sickness. It was common for our entire extended family to give affectionate hugs and kisses even when someone was ill. The belief of spreading germs was not in our conscious awareness and therefore, not given power.

When I reached my late teenage years and early twenties, I found myself exposed to many more universal beliefs. Part of my college studies involved health and wellness, and we were taught to accept so many of the health beliefs that gave power to sickness. Other beliefs were planted into my consciousness from daily interactions through work, general conversations and, of course, media. I progressively developed beliefs in many more powers other than the One that seemed to naturally be a part of me the first part of my life. We were all bombarded with these false powers, not just in health and wellness, but everything. This continued as my years passed by, especially working as a teacher in a public school. My illnesses or health issues increased in frequency and sometimes in severity. I could not figure out what was going on.

I now know the cause was the disappearance of my spiritual health and the development of a concession in universal beliefs. I was just like the Prodigal Son. As a youth, although I had no words for it, I was connected to the Father. His grace, love, and wisdom were my sufficiency. I truly had peace. Then, I ventured out into the adult world and lost my natural Oneness with him. The richness of My peace was cut off and soon depleted. Fortunately, I have found my way back home to the Father. You may ask then, "Have you seen a difference in your life, more specifically health and wellness?" Although it was not my goal or intention during my consciousness unfoldment, I clearly have noticed improved health being manifested in many ways. Nathanial Hawthorne succinctly states the truth of illness, "A bodily disease which we look upon as whole and entire within itself, may, after all, be but a symptom of some ailment in the spiritual part."

As we venture through Eden as being One with the Father, we will most likely experience various healings with ourselves and others. Once that realization of One Power grows in your consciousness, you will be amazed at the healings that occur. God's presence will show forth in the manifestation of health and wellness in the material world. The experience of knowing there is no separation between God and your self is such a blissful and liberating blessing from God. Spiritual health is the key to the fulfillment of all health. There is truth in spiritual healing when your consciousness transitions to the higher Christ state.

By no means am I advocating that we should avoid medical treatment. I am not saying we do not need modern medicine as we become one with God. Yes, our consciousness has transcended, but the majority of the human population consciousness has not. We cannot prevent the free will of others. There may still be accidents and illnesses due to the momentary rise of our ego or the free will of others in this world. Do not feel guilty, or as if it were a contradiction to our living in Eden concept if you seek or use medical care. The knowledge of modern medicine was instilled in us by God since the beginning, it just needed to be unraveled from our consciousness over time. Therefore, there is no wrongdoing in using modern medicine. Be alert though, that you do not err in forming a solitary dependence on modern medicine absent the development of spiritual health. The use of modern medical treatment can many times work well by itself, but the addition of spiritual health to medical treatment proliferates its effectiveness.

The reconstruction of our spiritual health enables our soul to expand and results in healing. We are not in pursuit of healing our body during our journey back to the Garden of Eden. The effort of awakening our spiritual health is not to alter or improve our material human body. The energy is used to transform our consciousness. This transformation into spiritual health or Christ Consciousness presents itself externally, as in this case, your supply for physical, mental and emotional health and wellness. Realize though, God's supply through spiritual health will come to you in whatever form you may need at that particular moment in time. God is omnipotent, omniscient and omnipresent.

> "Healing comes when the individual remembers his or her identity—the purpose chosen in the world of ancestral wisdom—and reconnects with that world of Spirit."
>
> —Malidoma Patrice Some

Leading Others to Eden

The joy of "My Peace" is strenuous to contain within you when you initially transform your consciousness. Your hope is that every person can live in the Garden of Eden with you as we are all heirs to the Father. Visions of heaven on earth come to your thoughts. How wonderful would that be, if every human on earth, especially your family and friends, lived life in the Garden? The desire to tell everyone you meet of your illumination is relentless at first. Remember though of the admonishment from chapter five about telling others. This is a secret and sacred relationship you have with God. It is not to be shouted from the mountain tops with verbal words and forced upon others. Your relationship is instead shouted from the mountain tops through the atmosphere of your divine Christ Consciousness. It needs no words, as God's presence with you shines so brightly, that those who are ready for It will see It with their true vision.

One reason you may yearn to teach others is that it may also help with your own contemplation on your relationship with God. Although it is not the purpose, the transformation of my consciousness to higher levels is one of the byproducts or benefits of me writing this book. That is why it is important to seek like-minded people or a spiritual teacher to contemplate together. The main reason you aspire to teach though is to bring the Christ Consciousness to the world. Those of us on this path should not discuss this with a person whose consciousness is ill prepared. When you usher the truth into an undeveloped spiritual consciousness of another, it will be met by a large roadblock. At best, you will get a confused but friendly smile, where you will see in their eyes that they do not truly understand. The conscious landscape of that particular person is not fertile. One cannot sow the seeds of truth into an infertile land. The concept of Eden will not take root and quickly disband into oblivion. Efforts of transforming consciousness will be futile in the consciousness of barren land. Force is a tool of the human ego, it is not God's will.

Although during the beginning of your journey into Eden, you keep your sacred relationship with the Lord that resides within private, you will still be able to attract others to the Garden of Eden. Focus as much as possible on being in a continuous state of Christ Consciousness. The central repeated action of God Consciousness that you display is the cornerstone for the consciousness rising in others. We start with our loved ones, our family and friends. Simply by being in the Christ Consciousness around them will many times cause an elevation in consciousness for them. You do not even need to say anything. This was true of Jesus. His presence alone, which was the presence of the Father because of his Christ Consciousness, illuminated those around him if they were ready. This was the case with the woman who was healed just by touching the cloak of Jesus in Mark 5:25-34. The presence of Christ in your consciousness becomes part of your home's atmosphere. This presence slowly slips into the consciousness of others without any realization of it. Barren land in your family becomes fertile, and soon the seeds of God's truth can be sowed. Do not force anything upon any family or friend. Those that are ready will come to you and will come to know their own Christ Consciousness.

This same action of living in Eden also will affect everyone who comes within the atmosphere of your consciousness's presence. This will be noticed everywhere. There will be complete strangers who will strike up a conversation with you like you have been friends forever. Some people may simply stare at you without being able to look away. There may be times that people thank you for helping them when you were not even attempting to help at that time. In this case, it is just the combination of the presence of your Christ Consciousness and the receptivity of their fertile spiritual soil. Sometimes these events will be obvious while other times it is discrete as in a simple look or smile. Those that are ready to transform their consciousness will come to you. They will recognize something about you, but not know what it is or how to describe it. For instance, my spiritual teachers did not know or pursue me. I also did not know them, but somehow our paths were connected as I was drawn to them. At the time, I recognized something indescribable within them, but could not pinpoint what that something was. I am now aware that the something that I intuitively recognized within them was God showing forth as my supply through my spiritual teachers. God was giving me exactly what I needed, when I needed it for the Father is omniscient.

At the risk of sounding egocentric, we must consciously bestow the Oneness with God or "My Peace" onto all that come in contact with us. You may call it blessing others with your Christ Consciousness. Do just as Jesus did, "Peace I leave with you, my peace I give unto you: not as the world giveth, give I unto you.", John 14:27. Your consciousness is being presented to anyone that comes into the atmosphere of your Christ awareness. This process must be a conscious bestowing on your part though. The peace of the Father is not passively given, it must be an active, silent and deliberate benediction. It can simply be done while driving or stopping into a convenience store for gas or wherever you may go. The physical place does not have to be exceptional or divine in some way or another for wherever you stand is holy ground.

Do not be fooled into thinking by blessing others with your Christ Consciousness that you are being egotistical. I am in no way saying you or I am above another. This is a form of God's grace showing forth in your consciousness onto others. It is not the human material form of I that is bestowing grace, it is the Father that resides within as One with all of us. We are the implement that God uses to bestow grace. "I can of mine own self do nothing…because I seek not mine own will, but the will of the Father which hath sent me.", John 5:30. Go forth and silently spread God's grace and love.

Flooding the consciousness with God's truth should not be forced onto any person. We are not here to judge others and their state of consciousness. God is the consciousness of every human. 2 Peter 1:3-4 informs us, "According as his divine power hath given unto us all things that pertain unto life and godliness, through the knowledge of him that hath called us to glory and virtue: Whereby are given unto us exceeding great and precious promises: that by these ye might be partakers of the divine nature, having escaped the corruption that is in the world through lust." If God is our consciousness, then all of God's truth is already within us. It is not up to you or me to unravel this truth and transform other's consciousness. This process is dependent upon the individual consciousness of each person. Trust that the consciousness of these individuals will properly guide them in proper time for them. We cannot remove the original sin of accepting the powers of good and evil. Yes, we can help if assistance is requested, but ultimately, the individual must do the arduous work themselves to gain access to the Garden of Eden. The way of the ego is easy and undisciplined, while the way to Eden is disciplined. "Enter ye in at the strait gate: for wide is the gate, and broad is the way, that leadeth to destruction, and many there be which go in there at: Because strait is the gate, and narrow is the way, which leadeth unto life, and few there be that find it.", Matthew 7:14-15.

Seekers will come to you when they are ready. Aspirants of the Christ Consciousness will be attracted or guided to you as you live in Eden. Do not be surprised when they seek you for healings, advice or teachings. Healing is usually the first path from which a seeker will connect with you. More often than not, a person beginning this spiritual path is conscious of something out of alignment within them, or possibly worse, feel as though they hit rock bottom in their life and cannot continue. He or she does not know what the error may be, but their intuition and spiritual health are beginning to develop and come forth. This is evident as they actively seek you for help. Besides mental, emotional and physical healing, advice will also be sought from you. Be aware of the advice you give. You must make sure the advice you offer is not centered upon your ego. If a person solicits advice on something you have no integrity or authority in, do not offer any. You must maintain your spiritual integrity by keeping the ego suppressed.

You may wonder, "What about all of the unconscious people in the world? How can I help them?" Again, just be One with God and consciously and silently share your Christ Consciousness with those that come into your domain. Those unconscious to their true identity should be dealt with absent of judgment or ridicule. Be compassionate and at the same time let them alone. Do not get into arguments, but do guard your peace found within, be silent and move on.

If a person is combative as you proceed on this path, do not give the situation any energy. There may be times that a previous relationship needs to end. Do not worry over this, for a relationship is not meant to be kept; it is meant to be enjoyed. If the relationship is chronically not appreciated and causes conflict, it is best to be discontinued. There are times it is helpful to ask yourself, "What is the gift or lesson of this person coming to me now?" Do not listen to the mind or ego making judgments of "he is an idiot" or "this person is hateful." Guilt may develop as feelings of anger arise in these situations. Guilt is the ego giving power to something other than God's omnipotence. It is perfectly fine to experience anger, just do not be bound to it. The story of Jesus and the moneychangers served as a great example of this. This story can be found in Matthew 21:12-17.

Go forth leading others to Eden by continuously living the Christ Consciousness. Focus on the present moment always bearing witness to God's presence. Bestow your consciousness on others in a sacred and silent way. Teach those that seek with spiritual integrity. Allow the natural spiritual health, that is inherently in every human, be revealed in its own due time. Simply live your true identity as One with God.

"You cannot help another who will not help him or herself. In the end, all souls must walk their path—and the reason they are walking a particular path may not be clear to us... or even to them at the level of ordinary human consciousness. Do what you can to help others, of course. Show love and caring whenever and wherever you can. But do not get caught up in someone else's 'story' to the point where you start writing it."

—Neale Donald Walsch

6

Realize, accept and live the fullness of God's
Omniscience. God is the One Mind and that
One Mind is your only Mind, not the human
mind or ego. It can never go away. Anything
that appears imperfect is merely evidence that
you are not yet convinced that the One Perfect
Mind of the Father is yours. The appearance
of imperfection is showing that you still
stray into believing in a second mind.

Christ and Christ Consciousness

A chapter on Christ was not originally going to be part of this book, but I have recently received two separate messages that this subject needs to be included for completeness. The first message was from my spiritual teacher, and the second was a confirmation of the needed message during a church sermon experience that contradicted the truth of God. Either way, the message came to me, I had no doubt, as I went within for the answer, that the Father wants me to address the topic of Christ. The absence or lack of understanding, by which many people possess, of what Christ and Christ Consciousness truly are is clearly visible all around us, including many churches. Christ can be a simple or complex concept to understand and live depending on your current level of consciousness. I know God's words will come from within, guiding this message as the topic of Christ is discussed and contemplated during this chapter.

What is Christ? Our quest for this answer must begin with ourselves, not looking outward. Sit in stillness and contemplate this question, "Who am I?" Are you merely a name that your earthly parents gave you? Are you a certain age or state of physical health? Are you the title of your occupation? Maybe you are that which you appear to be good at or bad at? This cannot be true, because then you are acknowledging good and evil within you, and we know that God is omnipotent, the only power. How about I'm faithful, a Christian, trustworthy, lovable, or any other descriptive. We must go much deeper than this. So, who are you? The "I" itself in you seems to be aware of many material perceptions or appearances, but the "I" itself is not aware of itself. What is the substance of this "I"? That is the key to the answer to our question, "What is Christ?". We must begin to remove the veil or blindfold that is obstructing our true vision and hearing.

This contemplation is the first step to uncovering who each one of us truly is. It helps you recognize what you are not. These questions help shatter and eliminate all misconceptions and in turn, remove the ego that controls us in the material world. The ego is not our true identity for it did not come from God. The ego acknowledges powers other than God, making us feel such things as fear. Fear causes us to manifest other emotions along the way such as jealousy, hatred and many others. By contemplating "Who am I?", you peel away the many layers of ego that encase the true I AM.

My intention is to help you find out the answer, but it is you that must unravel it from your consciousness and truly live it. Sit in stillness, meditate and look within. The answer is already there within you. Remember, "My kingdom is not of this world…", John 18:36. The material world lacks anything of God; the reality we perceive with our five senses in this world is just a mere misconception. In the dominion of truth or "My kingdom," there are no errors or ego. So, who do you believe you are? The only genuine answer is "I AM" or "I am the Christ." The Christ has always and will always be within each one of us. The divine reality of you and me is the Christ of you and me. We are each perfect in potential, but we are each not yet perfected.

You can only become what you already are. We can only learn what we already know. God has already given us every-thing we need. All we need to do is look within, for we are all heirs to the Father. Christ is the God feasibility in every person on earth. This is true not only for Christians but for all. Christ is the name given to our true identity as One with God. Christ is not one person like most think of as Jesus. Christ is a potential distinction that dwells within every human. We must commence by comprehending and acknowledging our "Christ potential," not by struggling to become righteous or spiritual. God has made us wholly spiritual from the beginning. This is a wonderful burden that is lifted from us when we awaken to the Christ within. One does not need to focus on following the Ten Commandments when they realize their Christ potential. The Christ that is in you guides your every movement keeping you living within the Kingdom of God where error or sin does not exist. It is no longer necessary to follow any list of rules to righteous living because your true divine self already lives and displays the righteous life as it is One with God. When you uncover your Christ Consciousness, the Ten Commandments are already a part of you.

Awareness of the presence of Christ or God within us is the true state of Grace. The coming of the Messiah in the Old Testament was not a man; it is the potential of each individual's Christ being brought forth into the individual's consciousness. The early Hebrews were blinded in the material world and took the Old Testament literally. They kept looking for a person to physically conquer those that kept them captive. Their consciousness was not ready to understand what the teachings of Jesus truly meant. Your Christ Consciousness is the Savior, your Savior. The Messiah is in each of us. This was misunderstood by many throughout the history of humans and is still so today. The Christ, Spirit or Soul is present within every individual of the past, present, and future. The Christ yearns to become One with your consciousness. Christ is waiting for your consciousness to wake up to the awareness of its presence within you.

Christ Consciousness is a spiritual consciousness, not a material consciousness. Each one of us must crucify all material sense of supply. Stop trying to improve human conditions, for we are not truly human. We are a soul, a spirit, heirs to the Father, One with God. We are the essence of God which is the Soul. When you believe in more than one power, God's omnipotence, you not only leave Eden, but you also crucify your Christ Consciousness.

During church today, I heard the pastor tell everyone, among the many other discrepancies between God's truth and the presence of ego during the sermon, that we are "not worthy." Do not ever listen to anyone, no matter what their material identity or position may be, that you are unworthy in any way, especially in the spiritual realm. This type of sermon is based on fear and is not rooted in God's truth. Do not feel unworthy of your true Christ potential or Christ Consciousness. This feeling of unworthiness is a sense of self apart from God. This sense of self apart from God must be crucified daily. We must all realize that we do not "have" anything. You or I don't "have" wisdom of God's truth. You are God's truth. I am God's truth. We are God's truth! This leads to the ascension of our Christ Consciousness and keeps us in the Garden of Eden.

Jesus was the master of the Christ potential or Christ Consciousness. There were many other before and many after Jesus that achieved a level of mastery, but no other soul achieved the ascension of Christ Consciousness in the material world at the level that Jesus demonstrated. Jesus said in John 8:12, "I am the light of the world: he that followeth Me shall not walk in darkness, but shall have the light of life." Was Jesus speaking of the human material form of Jesus when he said this? No, he knew better than anyone of his Oneness with the Father. He consciously realized his true divine identity that God and he could not be separated. Examine his words through the spiritual sense, not the material or literal senses.

The Christ lived so fully in Jesus that it was also demonstrated in his speech with words like "I", "Me" or "I am the Way." Jesus was not saying that only he was the Son of God.

Take notice of all of these types of pronouns and contemplate what Jesus is truly saying in John 10:28-36. "My sheep listen to My voice; I know them, and they follow Me. I give them eternal life, and they will never perish. No one can snatch them out of My hand. My Father who has given them to Me is greater than all. My Father who has given them to Me is greater than all. No one can snatch them out of My Father's hand. I and the Father are one." At this, the Jews again picked up stones to stone Him. But Jesus responded, "I have shown you many good works from the Father. For which of these do you stone Me?" "We are not stoning You for any good work," said the Jews, "but for blasphemy, because You, who are a man, declare Yourself to be God." Jesus replied, "Is it not written in your Law: 'I have said you are gods'?" If he called them gods to whom the word of God came—and the Scripture cannot be broken: then what about the One whom the Father sanctified and sent into the world? How then can you accuse Me of blasphemy' for stating that I am the Son of God?" Even the past students of Judaism and the Old Testament did not truly understand the level of Christ potential or Christ Consciousness in Jesus. They were focused on his words in the material sense of the world, not their true spiritual world.

There is no doubt that Jesus was the Christ and the Son of God, but so are each and every one of us. We are all One and not separate from God or each other. We are each like rays of light and the sun is like God. Although each ray of light travels forth from the sun, the light ray does not exist without its source, the sun. The light rays are all connected and one with the sun as we are with God. God does not favor one over another. "For God does not show favoritism.", Romans 2:11. Allow your savior, your Christ Consciousness, to unfold from within enabling you to reach your Christ potential. Master the eternal Christ that is you. Permit your Christ to be the light of the world bestowing God's grace wherever your human shadow may fall. Wherever you stand is holy ground. Do not be concerned what others think they know or preach. Be One with God, for One with God is a majority.

"In Absolute, Ultimate Reality, if you and all others were stripped of all personal concepts of consciousness, everyone would still be conscious, however, the consciousness would be universal consciousness, the mind of God, or God consciousness.

"Therefore, in an Absolute or Ultimate Reality, you and everyone else, although most would not have the least awareness of it, are God. As Christ put it, 'The Father and I are One.' And this is what is referred to metaphysically as Christ Consciousness, which is the same mentality or awareness that was in Christ, who recognized that ultimately all of life is an expression of the one universal life of God, or love."

—Dr. Paul Leon Masters, Theocentric Way of Life

Seven Keys to the Mastery of Christ Consciousness

7

Achieve the true "I AM" identity, attaining total fulfillment of One with God. Make the decision to go all of the way. Do not stand between the Spirit and Material worlds. Do not pause and be content. Go and show forth the full Glory of the Divine Image. Do not be satisfied and fall into the material trap. Do not make Spirit your servant, instead make yourself Spirit's servant. Mastership only comes to the one who makes Spirit their Master. There are infinite mansions in God's Kingdom. There is no place to stop unfolding while attaining Divine Righteousness.

The Dream of Reality

*A*n interesting question was posed to me last night before my ten-year-old daughter went to bed. My daughter asked, "Daddy, did you ever think that the life we are living is just a dream, and we are already in Heaven?" This question came out of the blue with no promptings from me, and it took me by surprise a bit. All I could say at that moment was, "Yes. Yes, I have." She was satisfied with my response and went on her way to bed. I was amazed at the deepness of her inquiry and thought that this question should be explored a bit in our journey to the Garden of Eden. What a wonderful example of how God's truth and knowledge are already in us even at a young age.

What is life? What is the force that can create life? Is life possible without it? These questions are good starting points for this topic. Jesus says in John 8:58, "…before Abraham was born, I Am!" The Father was the beginning of all creation. God is the invisible spiritual force that creates and sustains life. Without God's life force, there would be no life. This force was here before the first human was created and will always be here. Again, without the Father, there is no life. One might say that God is eternal and immortal life.

Can we truly describe what God is though? Our mortal mind or ego can come up with many renditions of God, but is the ego capable of discerning God's image and God's omniscient, omnipotent and omnipresent characteristics? The best description the human ego can come up with is some sort of image based off of its own material senses and the teachings learned from other egos. The description I hear the most is "God is love." The best description I have ever heard is simply, "God Is." It is beyond our human mind to be able to comprehend what the Lord truly is. God is not part of our material world, God is spiritual. We cannot sense God with our material world senses. The Father's kingdom is a spiritual kingdom, therefore requires spiritual senses.

Genesis 1:27 tells us, "So God created man in his own image, in the image of God created he him; male and female created he them." That scripture gives us the answer to our identity. Again, God cannot be perceived by the five material senses of sight, hearing, smell, taste, and touch. If we cannot perceive God with our five senses, and God created us in his image, how can we perceive ourselves? Our physical body is not in God's likeness because it can be perceived by the five material world senses. Our true identity cannot be known through these senses. Pema Chodron described this perfectly when she said, "We are spiritual beings having a human experience."

We know that the Father manifested himself as us, therefore we are One with God. The relationship between God's life force and our life is described in John 15:5-6, "I am the vine;

you are the branches. If you remain in me and I in you, you will bear much fruit; apart from me you can do nothing. If you do not remain in me, you are like a branch that is thrown away and withers; such branches are picked up, thrown into the fire and burned." We are never disconnected from God's life force. If there were no God, there would be no life force, and we would not exist as spiritual beings or souls. A branch cannot live apart from a tree. The branch and tree are one entity. Indian spiritual leader Sathya Sai Baba describes our relationship with God as "I am you; you are ME. You are the waves; I am the ocean. Know this and be free, be divine." God is the ocean and we are the waves. A wave is not separate from the ocean; it is one with the ocean.

The Tree of Knowledge of good and evil is the oldest illusion of mankind's ego. It is the original error or all errors. This illusion allows our mortal mind or ego to manifest the acceptance of two worlds, two powers. One world is recognized and perceived by our five senses. This is the material world that most consider reality; the world that dismisses you from the Garden of Eden. Since we know our true identity cannot be perceived with material senses, because we are made in God's image; we are therefore spiritual just as our Lord is. The true spiritual world of our being can only be discerned when our spiritual senses or Christ Consciousness is developed. Instead of only accepting that our true world is the spiritual kingdom of God, we allow the Tree of Knowledge's illusion of multiple powers to hypnotize our consciousness into believing the material world is reality. This material world and its five senses is not our true reality, as Jesus said, "I am in this world, but not of it." As the belief in two powers gives way and vanishes, so does the dream that the material world is our reality.

Everything you think of yourself as being your identity is your ego telling you a story. It is an illusion of reality. Ego creates the material world in varied ways. Your ego ranks and judges everything on the belief of the powers of good and evil. The ego's material world is a hallucination; it is not true reality. This does not mean we are to be lazy in this material human world. We must hold fast to the truth of being One with God. This takes strict discipline as the path to Eden is straight and narrow. Laziness leads to acceptance of the two powers of good and evil. Since most cannot perceive their true spiritual identity as One with God, most perceive themselves as mortal and error in the belief of material powers.

The ego's manifested illusion in the human mind cannot be personified external to the mind. Considering the hallucination is rooted in the human mind, the error of the hallucination cannot be rectified external the mind. We must go within to correct the error. Only with our inner true vision can we see the spiritual identity of ourselves and others. One whose consciousness is not spiritually developed cannot see this, for one is fixed in the world of material consciousness. Marianne Williamson helped us understand by saying, "In our natural state, we are glorious beings. In the world of illusion, we are lost and imprisoned slaves to our appetites and our will to false power."

The true dream or illusion is not being capable of perceiving and understanding that our world is truly divine, spiritual in nature and eternal. This is the only true world which is always present and governs as God's law. The dream is not that the material human world does not exist. It exists, just not as the true kingdom of our spiritual being or our true identity as immortal souls adjoined with God. If you do your research, you will see that modern science is now beginning to agree with the concept of the eternal soul. Solicit nothing from the material dream world most perceive as reality. Searching for something from this dream state is only searching for an improved dream. It will not improve your reality in the spiritual realm. Awaken from your slumber and rid yourself of the dream. Seek only a relationship with the Father as One with God.

We know our physical bodies and material world are not spiritual. God is spiritual, and therefore our souls are spiritual, immortal and everlasting. If our bodies and the physical world were spiritual, they would not change or perish over time. We would not get sick or hurt. We would not grow old. This is clearly not the case as we experience the aging process on the human plane. Our material selves and world are not the substance or life force of God. Our souls, the spiritual true identities of each of us, are from God and therefore eternal and immortal. Our soul is the divine true identity of us that chooses to have a human life, so it may experience from another perspective and learn. Do the work by going within to discover the Christ potential within you. Develop your Christ Consciousness to its fullest, and in turn, you will dissolve the ego's hallucination of believing the material world as reality.

The soul is an individual copy of the Creator, God. The soul and the Father are One, just as the wave and the ocean are one. If God is omnipresent, and we are made in the Lord's image and are One with God, then we are also omnipresent. Therefore, we are present everywhere at the same time. By this nature, we can answer the original question posed by my daughter with, "Yes, we are on earth and heaven at the same time, as we are also already in the Garden of Eden."

> "Do not be misled by what you see around you or be influenced by what you see. You live in a world which is a playground or illusion, full of false paths, false values and false ideas. But, you are not part of that world."
>
> —Sathya Sai Baba

Crucify Your Ego

*B*efore my wife and I were married we attended a pre-marriage counseling session with the pastor who was to wed us. The main message the pastor told us was we are to die for each other daily. We were advised to let our personal wants and desires to die or sacrifice them or set them aside for what is best for our spouse. My wife and I had some fun with this when we partook in some sort of sacrifice for the other pointing out at times that "I am dying for you right now." It was good advice for a young couple entering marriage but let us take this concept further and apply it to our return to the Garden of Eden.

So now we begin the most difficult part of this journey. We each must crucify the personal sense of thoughts, words, mind, life, health, companionship, supply, body, etc. Our egos must be crucified daily. Our egos are great imitators of the still small voice of God within. It is necessary to be able to distinguish between the two. We must crucify our egos or personal sense of awareness every moment of every day as we are bombarded with the appearance of error or lack.

Joel S. Goldsmith suggested that we always have an attitude of listening. Not listening to others but listening to God within. Do not engage in thought. Instead, stand still listening for the Word of God. This can be a hearing of actual words, just a knowing, a vision, a tingling or other indescribable experience. You just know that at that moment God is consciously within you. Joel suggested practicing being still with no thought of mind for thirty to sixty seconds, twelve times per day. At the beginning of your journey, this process of practicing is usually done with your eyes closed, but eventually, you will develop the ability to practice God's presence with your eyes open.

Begin the exercise of the crucifixion of ego not only during the appearance of discordance, such as disease, sin or any appearance of error, makes itself known, but also when appearances of harmony and good will arise. We must remove the human mind, the personal sense of awareness or material world out of the depiction or appearance by crucifying it. As we begin this journey, we usually begin with using statements of truth as crutches to negate error. As your consciousness evolves you must go further than this. Do not state or repeat truths. Crucify your personal sense! Realize that you do not know the truth, you are the truth, I AM the truth. I AM the way. Work towards being in stillness and in receptiveness to the Father within even when your eyes are open, or you are engaged in a conversation with another.

This is difficult to do, especially as your consciousness is new to this transformation of your Christ potential. One strategy I used and still do at times now was to ask the following questions to myself. Who is the "I" that is experiencing an appearance of an error or emotion at this very moment? Is it my true "I" or spiritual self or is the "I" my ego? Who is being offended or hurt at this moment of the appearance of error? Whenever having difficulty with an error, the answer is it is always my ego, not my true spiritual self that is heir to God.

The Lord is always working out his spiritual plan through us. We need to understand that we can relax and learn to be a beholder to God's guidance. What we think is our personal life is not ours. It is God's life unfolding individually. Our egos must step aside and be crucified or else we will give birth to a material personal sense of awareness. This will then lead to living a mortal material life. This mortal material life must die. It must be crucified! Take no thought of what your ego desires in the material world. We cannot serve ego and God, only God is to be served. Contemplate and go within on what Matthew 24-30 is telling us. "No man can serve two masters: for either he will hate the one, and love the other; or else he will hold to the one, and despise the other. Ye cannot serve God and mammon. Therefore I say unto you, Take no thought for your life, what ye shall eat, or what ye shall drink; nor yet for your body, what ye shall put on. Is not the life more than meat, and the body than raiment? Behold the fowls of the air: for they sow not, neither do they reap, nor gather into barns; yet your heavenly Father feedeth them. Are ye not much better than they? Which of you by taking thought can add one cubit unto his stature? And why take ye thought for raiment? Consider the lilies of the field, how they grow; they toil not, neither do they spin: And yet I say unto you, That even Solomon in all his glory was not arrayed like one of these. Wherefore, if God so clothe the grass of the field, which today is, and tomorrow is cast into the oven, shall he not much more clothe you, O ye of little faith?"

Every time the appearance of lack or discord is recognized you must immediately stop reacting to it. Do not act out towards the appearance. Immediately turn within to stillness and listen. Remember this practice must also be executed in the appearance of good in the material world, not just the bad or lack. Only God is good. Say for instance you come across a sum of money, do not think what the money can do for you. This would be taking thought of your ego and personal sense of awareness. Instead go within and listen for the Father's message. Father what should I do with this gift that has resulted as an effect of your spiritual supply?

Living in the material, world while worshipping your ego, leads to power being given to error. Yes, we say that error has no power, but that is only true when an individual reaches the Christ Consciousness. An error has no power in the illumined, impersonal consciousness that is One with God. A personal sense of self cannot crucify a personal sense of self. In other words, the ego cannot rid the ego. The personal sense of awareness can only be crucified on a spiritual level, the level of your true identity as heir of the Father. Each one of us must turn within to listen to the Father and take no thought. It is always God's grace, love and good pleasure that will express as our experiences as you make your ego step aside. At your will Lord, convey thyself at this moment and time. At this point, God will make known his sense of supply, not a personal or material sense of supply. Become fully aware that you are One with God, therefore you can realize to yourself that "I AM supply." Our spiritual identity as Sons of God is the only supply we need.

This brings us to another topic that deals with crucifying your personal sense of self, forgiveness. Jesus said in Matthew 18:21-22, "Then came Peter to him, and said, Lord, how oft shall my brother sin against me, and I forgive him? till seven times? Jesus saith unto him, I say not unto thee, Until seven times: but, Until seventy times seven." Forgiveness is crucifying the personal sense of self, the ego. It is taking away the duality of judgment and two powers, for only God is omnipotent. Forgiveness is not done for the other person. Realize this and remove the duality of the ego's mortal mind. Take the stance of saying this to yourself, "Father, forgive me for I have misjudged your creation. Forgive me for I have sat in judgment upon them. Forgive that I have hated, envied or errored them in any way. Forgive me for using my mortal eyes to see instead of using my true sight."

There are times it is difficult to crucify the ego and forgive. When this appearance of difficulty forgiving arises, ask God to forgive for you. A good starting point will be, "Father, I cannot forgive at this moment as I am having difficulty shedding my material personal sense of self. Please forgive for me. Lord, at thy will, let thy grace, love and wisdom flow forth in this present moment." Then sit in silence and let God flow through you in stillness. God's grace will then lead you to be able to shed the ego and truly forgive in proper time.

Forgiveness is not viewing a person who has done you wrong and then thinking of forgiving them out of the generosity of your human heart. This is not crucifying your personal sense of self. Your ego is front and center when you convey this stance. You are not a martyr by forgiving. Forgiveness is the ability to recognize that the appearance of an error is the ego showing yourself a personal awareness and material picture. Be willing to crucify that personal sense of ego and go into stillness within to use your true sight. Keep your true eyes wide open. Ask the Father what the unconditional Christ Consciousness sees, what the mortal mind cannot see. This act of stillness is an ongoing process for forgiveness. Continue practicing it with your eyes shut, then open until you reach the consciousness of Jesus.

Do not forgive people. Forgive yourself for at any point entertaining your ego, personal, material or conditioned sense of mind. Forgiveness is not a tool to show you are a righteous person. We are not attempting to be a better person. We are attempting to become the Christ. Forgiveness is a tool or way to reach the Christ Consciousness while developing a true relationship with God.

We cannot serve two powers. Only God is omnipotent, omniscient and omnipresent. Matthew 6:21-24 tells us, "For where your treasure is, there will your heart be also. The light of the body is the eye: if therefore thine eye be single, thy whole body shall be full of light. But if thine eye be evil, thy whole body shall be full of darkness. If therefore the light that is in thee be darkness, how great is that darkness! No man can serve two masters: for either he will hate the one, and love the other; or else he will hold to the one, and despise the other. Ye cannot serve God and mammon."

Crucify your personal sense of self, your ego! This is the most difficult part of this journey. It takes great discipline and practice. "Except the Lord build the house, they labour in vain that build it: except the Lord keep the city, the watchman waketh but in vain. It is vain for you to rise up early, to sit up late, to eat the bread of sorrows: for so he giveth his beloved sleep. Lo, children are an heritage of the Lord: and the fruit of the womb is his reward. As arrows are in the hand of a mighty man; so are children of the youth. Happy is the man that hath his quiver full of them: they shall not be ashamed, but they shall speak with the enemies in the gate.", Psalm 127. Spiritual supply brings joy, peace, and harmony. Spiritual supply is gained through crucifying your ego. This is what is needed to enter the Garden of Eden. First and foremost, always seek the Kingdom of God, never seek the kingdom of ego!

“Zen says that if you drop knowledge—and within knowledge, everything is included; your name, your identity, everything, because this has been given to you by others—if you drop all that has been given by others, you will have a totally different quality to your being: innocence. This will be a crucifixion of the persona, the personality, and there will be a resurrection of your innocence. You will become a child again, reborn. "

—Acharya Rajneesh

Welcome to Eden

*A*t this time, I would like to welcome each of you back to the Garden of Eden, your true home. Some of you may have already realized your Christ within, your Oneness with God and have been in Eden for quite some time. Others of you are similar to where I am on this unfoldment. You are either just beginning your journey or are in the middle or end of the voyage to fulfilling your Christ potential. Nine short months ago, the material or human form of me would never have imagined I would be writing this book, or even speaking about spiritual truth or scripture. It was not on my radar. Family, friends, and others that know me will most likely be bewildered that the words and thoughts in this book came from me; for to them, I am just a common man, a public-school teacher, or any other material descriptive their ego portrays me as. Then again, did these concepts come from me, or did they come from a higher source? Just like in John 5:30, "I can of mine own self do nothing." It is the Christ within that wrote this book. The human I was only the implement as the still small voice of God directed my earthly actions from within. This book was not done by my will, but instead, it was done by the Father's will.

The Christ deep within me woke up my consciousness with no warning. The immaculate conception of my Christ Consciousness took place. As you may already know, this entire process of Christ Consciousness evolution is such a liberation, and it is a true blessing of God's grace.

The transformation of consciousness back to Eden is a continuous process. The path is straight and narrow; therefore, it takes constant work and practice. This is not a lazy path. It is a way of living, the natural way of living as God intended. You are the living Christ, heir to God. I stress this again, as long as you listen to the Father within, the Lord will lead you down the spiritual and righteous path. There is no strenuous effort needed in following the Ten Commandments, for you are One with God. The intention of this book is to help you in the undertaking of shedding your human identity and being born anew with your Christ Consciousness.

In Eden, you will recognize and eliminate the error of human universal beliefs. This includes religious, governmental, medical or any other type of universal law made from the ego of man and forced upon us for thousands of years. God is the only law, and this law resides within each of us. Eliminate the ego, that human "I" from your consciousness. Only God is good, for this reason, our material form cannot do good. There is only one power, for the Father is omnipotent, omniscient and omnipresent. Jesus informed us of this feat in John 16:33, "I have overcome the world." This was Jesus saying that he shed his ego, his material identity, and the material world, so that only his true spiritual identity, Christ, remained. This freed him from the belief in two powers. The material Jesus was no longer there to experience appearances of good or bad. Only the Christ was left to fulfill God's will.

Recall that temptations will arise in us. The ego will stand up here and there, but you will quickly remember you are One with God. The ego will then bow down realizing there is only One power, and you are truly the Son of God. Do not agonize or fret that you have not attained a sufficient transformation in Christ Consciousness. God meets each of us at the level of consciousness we are currently living. God's spiritual supply is sufficient for the current moment in time. It is not sufficient for the future or past, only the present time. As you live your current Christ potential, you realize God's gifts in every moment. You do not attempt to seize illumination at any point in time. This illumination will manifest into your consciousness when you are ready, not before or after. God's grace, love, and wisdom is your sufficiency at this hour, not the next.

This can also be said about prayer, which is another topic for a book of its own. In Eden, there is no use to pray for any material object or human good. God is omniscient, and God does not favor one person over the other. God already knows what you need, when you need it. One cannot influence the Father for he is omnipotent. One cannot escape the Lord for he is omnipresent. Your only prayer is simply consciously realizing your true nature as the Christ, Son of God, One with God. Praying any other way that asks for any material thing or concept is simply the human ego trying to influence God. Sitting in stillness contemplating your Oneness with God, that Christ is the Soul of man, is true prayer. The nature of prayer is to truly know God and have a relationship as One with him, not to ask for anything.

The development of Christ Consciousness will not strip you of your individual personality. You cannot take away what you already are, for each one of us is a unique and infinite expression of God. If anything, you are now realizing you are truly free to express your true individuality because you live under God's law, not the laws of ego and universal beliefs. The truth of your divine spiritual identity will indeed set you free.

Do not feel as though you need to be or appear as a stereotypical holy person as you live life in the Garden of Eden on earth. Your soul, your Christ wants you to enjoy your experiences. The Father has given each of us everything we need to experience His peace. I encourage you to still keep your sense of humor and adventure in life. For the human life is an adventure for our souls. Enjoy the pleasures and relationships that come to you, but do not rely on them. Stay rooted in the fact that every one of us is divine. Material errors may still happen to those of us on this path, for we cannot stop the free will of those that worship two powers and false idols of the material world. We can though consciously understand that these errors have no power. Jesus said, "The kingdom of God is within you." We do not look outward to find God, nor do we look to God to obtain power. By living God's peace that is the inner presence of us, we can be whole while enjoying a full life of joy, harmony and spiritual abundance.

I or no other spiritual person or teacher can delivery you to Eden. We cannot help those that will not help themselves in this transformation of consciousness. Every individual, every soul or spirit must take their own journey to Eden, to the Father within. God is always communing with us. Are you listening to the Lord? We do not need to change anything in the material world, but we do need to transition our consciousness from the material to the spiritual. Seeing is not believing. Instead, know that believing in your Christhood is truly seeing. The greatest gift you can give yourself if to expand your Christ Consciousness and realize your true "I AM" identity. Your Christ is everywhere just as Saint Patrick described, "Christ be with me, Christ within me, Christ behind me, Christ before me, Christ beside me, Christ to comfort me and restore me, Christ beneath me, Christ above me, Christ in quiet, Christ in danger, Christ in hearts of all that love me, Christ in mouth of friend and stranger."

Go forth in Eden and live your Christ potential while still being in this world, but not being of it. Unceasingly commune with God. Every one of us is our own Savior. We are each the Messiah and the second coming of the Christ. You already are who you are looking for. You are deserving no matter what others may say or how they may attempt to refute this truth. Release your Christ potential. God manifests himself as us. In turn, God is us, therefore we are One. Be One with God!

Welcome home to Eden my friends!

"You are the luminous mystery in which the entire universe with its forms and phenomena arises and subsides. When this realization dawns there is a complete transformation of your personal self into your universal self…the complete loss of all fear, including death. You have become a being who radiates love the same way the sun radiates light. You have finally arrived at the place from which your journey begins."

—Deepak Chopra